A T

I want to say Thank You for buying my book so I put together a free gift for you!

This gift is the perfect complement to this book so just visit the link below to get access.

www.GoodLivingPublishing.com/glutenitalian

Contents

Introduction

One of my favorite styles of cooking is Italian but in the world of gluten-free eating finding simple and delicious recipes isn't always that easy. There is nothing worse than wanting to cook one of your favorite Italian dishes but realizing it calls for a lot of gluten! This book will ensure that never happens to you again… only delicious, gluten-free Italian recipes from now on

Now you may choose to avoid gluten as you're intolerant or maybe it's for health benefits (of which there are many), but having to avoid your favorite Italian dish is something I never want you to have to go through again.

With these recipes, you can include delicious pizzas, risottos, pastas and much, much more in your life safe in the knowledge that it won't wreak havoc on your body or your diet.

Not only that but I have also whipped you up recipes for delicious gluten-free gelatos and desserts. Satisfy that sweet tooth of yours and enjoy eating 100% guilt free.

Every recipe in this book has been kept as simple as possible. You won't find any difficult steps or uncommon terms.

I wrote this book to make cooking Italian food as quick and easy as possible without any compromise on taste. Some recipe books make things more complicated than they need to be. This book strips all the complexity away and leaves you with short and easy to follow recipes that are all absolutely delicious. Even most of the recipes have English names so you know exactly what you're cooking. That said I've left a few Italian names in, but only the simple ones!

So get your apron on and heat up the pans because you have a whole book of new delicious Italian recipes to taste.

Happy cooking!

Love,

Sarah Sophia

Starter Recipes

Classic Italian Bruschetta

Ingredients: Serves 4-6

Gluten free bread – 8 slices
4 large tomatoes (heirloom are best but you can others if you like)
2 cloves of fresh garlic, minced
1 avocado
1 cup of basil, finely chopped
The juice from half of a lemon
2 tbsp of olive oil
Salt and pepper to your taste

Directions

Heat your oven to 375F

Place 6-8 slices of bread on a non-stick baking sheet. Brush with oil and place in the oven.

Cook for 3 - 5 minutes until golden with a slight browning on the edges.

Take the toast from the oven and allow to cool on a plate.

Dice the avocado and the tomatoes and Place them in a large mixing bowl

Add the basil, lemon juice, olive oil, salt and pepper, and toss everything until well mixed together.

Spoon the mixture over the toast and serve.

Ingredients: Serves 4

3 zucchinis
Sea salt, to taste
5 cloves of garlic, minced or finely chopped
Ground black pepper, to taste
2 tbsp olive oil
8 oz. mozzarella, torn or sliced
3 Heirloom tomatoes, sliced
1.5 tsp chopped basil
1 cup Crunchy Gluten Free Bread Crumbs

Directions

Preheat the oven to 370F.

Chop the ends of the zucchini. Cut in half and slice lengthwise into thin, flat strips.

Lay strips on paper towel, one under one on top, and press to extract moisture. Remove top paper towel and sprinkle with salt.

In a small oven proof dish layer the strips in an overlapping pattern.

Season with pepper and garlic.

Add a layer of mozzarella slices and drizzle with oil.

Add a layer of tomatoes. Season with salt, pepper and chopped basil.

Final layer is made up of the bread crumbs. Sprinkle over ensuring an even coating.

Bake for 35 minutes. Should be golden brown on top.

Simple & Delicious Focaccia

Ingredients: Serves 4-6

2.5 cups of speciality flour mix (see below)
1 tbsp xanthan gum
1 tsp salt
¾ tsp pepper
1 tsp crushed rosemary
1 tsp oregano
2 tbsp sugar
1.5 cups warm water
2 tbsp yeast
1 tsp sugar
2 tbsp olive oil
2 medium/large eggs

Directions

Take the first 7 dry ingredients and add to a bowl, mix to combine them and set aside.

Combine half of the water, the yeast, and 1 teaspoon of sugar in a mixing bowl. Wait for the yeast to proof and become foamy. Add the remainder of the water, the olive oil, and the eggs.

Using the flat beater attachment of a mixer, mix the ingredients from step 2 on low and then add the reserved flour mixture all at once. Mix this on low speed until no lumps remain in the bowl. The dough should now resemble a thick batter.

Grease a baking tray, add the dough and press evenly to form a thick crust. Allow this to rise uncovered in a warm place, until it doubles in bulk.

Preheat the oven 425F.

Before baking top with caramelized onions.

Bake for 25-30 minutes until golden brown.

Speciality Flour Mix
5 lbs. flour. Must be white rice flour.
30 oz. potato starch, be careful as this is not the same as potato flour.

Ingredients: Serves 4-6

1.5 cup sifted almond flour
¾ cup arrowroot powder
¼ cup golden flax meal
½ tsp salt
½ tsp sodium bicarbonate
4 eggs
1 tsp honey
1 tsp apple cider vinegar
¼ cup walnuts roughly chopped
¼ cup hazelnuts roughly chopped
½ cup pistachios roughly chopped
¼ cup pumpkin seeds
¼ cup sunflower seeds
¼ cup sesame seeds

Directions

Preheat your oven to 350F and oil a loaf pan.

In a mixing bowl combine the flour, flax meal, salt, arrowroot and sodium bicarbonate. Mix well.

Using a separate bowl blend the eggs until frothy. Add the honey and vinegar, stir everything well.

Combine the two bowls and mix all the ingredients together. Stir well for 1 minute.

Take your load pan and pour the batter in.

Bake for thirty five minutes.

Pistachio Nut & Spinach Pesto Spread

Ingredients: Serves 4-6

2 tbsp olive oil
¼ cup white onion, diced
2 cloves garlic, minced
5 cups of fresh spinach
2 tbsp nutritional yeast
¾ cup pistachio nuts
Sea salt to taste

Directions

Take a large pan and add the oil, onions and garlic and cook for 2-3 minutes over a medium heat.

Add the spinach and cook until spinach is well wilted.

Take off the heat and spoon the spinach mixture into a food processor. Add the remaining ingredients as well.

Mix until smooth.

Transfer to a serving bowl.

Serve on gluten-free crackers, gluten-free oatcakes or a spread on toast.

Ingredients: Serves 4-6

2 quarts gluten-free chicken stock
2 tbsp olive oil
3 cloves of garlic, minced
1 onion, finely chopped
2 medium carrots, skinned and sliced
4 gluten-free Italian sausages, chopped into chunks
1 tsp dried oregano
1 tbsp dried basil
¼ cup fresh parsley, chopped
2 cups uncooked white rice
½ cup cream

Directions

Take a large pot and heat the oil over a medium heat. Add the garlic and onions and sauté until the onions become translucent.

Add the sausages and cook until well browned on all sides.

Add the stock, oregano, basil and parsley. Bring to a boil, then reduce heat to low and simmer for an hour.

Add the carrots and rice. Bring to the boil, reduce heat and let it simmer for 25 minutes.

Remove from heat and stir in cream before serving.

Ingredients: Serves 4

4 tbsp olive oil
2 leeks, sliced
4 carrots, chopped coarsely
2 zucchinis, sliced thinly
8 oz. green beans, cut into pieces
4 stalks of celery, chopped
6 cabbage leaves, chopped
3 quarts gluten-free chicken or vegetable stock
2 pounds chopped tomatoes (use large tomatoes)
2 tbsp fresh thyme, chopped
2 cans of cannellini, or white beans, with liquid
½ cup of red wine, I prefer a darker wine
Salt and ground black pepper to taste

Directions

Heat the olive oil in a large pot over a medium to high heat.

Add the carrots, leeks, zucchini, green beans, and celery. Cover the pot and the reduce heat to low. Cook for 15 minutes, stirring the pan occasionally to avoid burning the veg.

Add the stock, cabbage, tomatoes, thyme and beans, along with their liquid. Bring everything to a boil then reduce the heat and cover with lid. Let it simmer for around 30 minutes, stirring occasionally.

Add the red wine, stir well and then continue to let it simmer for 15 minutes.

Remove the pot from heat, and allow it cool slightly.

Season with salt and pepper.

Serve with grated pecorino Romano cheese and a little parsley

Spiced Sausage & Bean Soup

Ingredients: Serves 4

½ pound of Italian sausage
1 onion chopped finely
1 tbsp garlic, minced
2 tbsp olive oil
1 can cannellini beans
6 cups gluten-free chicken stock
Hot pepper flakes or similar spice
½ head of escarole, thinly chopped
Black pepper
Parmesan cheese, grated

Directions

Preheat oven to 425F.

Oil a baking tray and put the sausages in oven until cooked through and well browned.

Remove sausages from the oven, let them cool and then cut into chunks.

Add ½ cup of chicken stock to the baking tray and use a spatula to scrape off any browned pieces of sausage from the pan. You will use this later in the soup.

Take a large pot and place over a medium heat and add the olive oil.

Add the onions and sauté until translucent, usually this takes 3-4 minutes. Add the garlic and cook for further 1-2 minutes. Make sure they are well mixed.

Add the chicken stock (and the half cup of stock from the roasting pan), the beans, sausage chunks and pepper flakes.

Bring to the boil and then turn heat down and let it simmer for 30 minutes.

Whilst the soup is simmering away beautifully, chop your escarole. Add this to the soup and stir.

Cook for a further 20-30 minutes stirring occasionally. The escarole should start to break apart slightly and separate. If the soup begins to look too thick, add more stock.

Serve with grated parmesan cheese.

Ingredients: Serves 4-6

6 large eggs
1 bunch of asparagus, chopped (remove the ends and dispose)
1.5 cups gluten-free marinara sauce
1 tablespoon olive oil
1 clove garlic, finely chopped
2 cups gluten-free chicken broth
¼ cup fresh grated Pecorino Romano

Directions

Put a large pan over a medium heat and add the olive oil. As the oil begins to heat add the garlic and cook until slightly brown. Should take 1-2 minutes.

Pour in the marinara sauce and then the chicken broth, stir well.

Add asparagus pieces, stir and then cover the pan until the sauce begins to boil.

When the sauce boils reduce the heat to low. Gently crack your eggs you eggs and add on top of sauce. Just as if you were making a fried egg.

Sprinkle cheese on top.

Simmer on low for 10 minutes

Sautéed Red Peppers Set in a Caper Sauce

Ingredients: Serves 4

1.5 pounds red bell peppers, use 3 – 4 medium sized peppers
3 tablespoons olive oil
¼ cup water
2 tsp white-wine vinegar
2 tbsp capers, chopped (liquid drained)
¼ tsp sugar

Directions

Cut each pepper into long pieces, remove the stems and seeds and discard.

Heat 1 tbsp oil in a pan over a medium heat and add chopped peppers with ½ tsp of salt and pepper for about 5 minutes.

Turn heat to low, add the water and continue to cook peppers for 15 minutes, or until the liquid evaporates.

Whilst the peppers cook. Take the remaining 2 tbsp of oil, vinegar, capers, sugar and add to a large bowl and mix well. Pour the caper sauce into the pan with the peppers and mix well.

Salt and Pepper to taste.

Classic Tomato & Mozzarella Salad

Ingredients: Serves 2

6 large tomatoes, roughly cut and cubed
2 tbsp balsamic vinegar
½ cup fresh basil, chopped
2 tbsp olive oil
12 oz. buffalo mozzarella cheese
Basil for garnishing
Sea salt & Black pepper

Directions

Toss the tomatoes in a large bowl with 1 tbsp of vinegar. Coat well.

Add the basil and 1 tbsp of olive oil. Sprinkle with salt and pepper. Toss everything again, ensuring to coat well.

Take the tomato mixture and mound it in the centre of your serving plate(s).

Roughly cut or tear the mozzarella cheese into small – medium pieces and place them decoratively over the tomato.

Drizzle the salad with 1 tbsp of olive oil and season with salt and pepper to taste.

Use the basil sprigs as garnish.

With the remaining 1 tbsp of vinegar drizzle it around the plate before service.

Main Course Recipes

Lasagne

Ingredients: Serves 4-6

1 package gluten-free lasagne noodles (8 oz.)
½ pound ground pork sausage
½ pound ground beef
2 cloves of garlic, minced
1 medium onion, finely diced
1 can diced tomatoes
1 can tomato paste (6 oz.)
2 tsp dried parsley
1 tsp dried basil
1 tsp dried oregano
1 pinch white sugar
8 oz. sour cream
8 oz. of ricotta cheese
3 eggs, lightly beaten
1.5 pounds of mozzarella cheese, shredded or roughly cut
1 cup grated pecorino Romano cheese
2 tsp salt
½ tsp ground black pepper

Directions

Heat oven to 375F

Cook the lasagne noodles in a pot of boiled water with 1 tbsp of oil (check cooking instructions on the pack of noodles).

Heat a large pan over medium-high heat. Add a 1 tbsp of olive oil and cook the onions until they begin to become translucent.

At this point add the sausage, beef and garlic. Cook until the meat is all well browned. Be sure to drain off any excess fat.

Add the diced tomatoes, tomato paste, parsley, basil, oregano, and sugar. Stir well for 1 minute.

Increase the heat and bring to a boil. Once boiling point is reached reduce the heat to low. Let it simmer for about 25 minutes, stirring occasionally. The sauce will begin to thicken during this time.

Take a large bowl and mix the eggs, sour cream, ricotta, Romano cheese, salt, black pepper, and half of the mozzarella cheese.

To make the lasagne, add a thin layer of the cooked sauce over the bottom of a baking pan. Layer ⅓ of the lasagne noodles on top of the sauce. Then add ⅓ of the remaining sauce and ⅓ of the cream mix. Repeat this layering 2 more times.

Sprinkle the remaining mozzarella cheese over top of the lasagne. If any sauce remains, feel free to drizzle this atop as well.

Bake for 30 minutes at 375F. The sauce should be bubbling and the cheese should be golden brown.

Ingredients: Serves 2

2 fillets of any white fish
3 tbsp pine nuts, chopped or crushed
2 tbsp parmesan cheese, grated
¼ tsp minced garlic or one clove chopped finely
1 tsp basil pesto
1.5 tbsp mayonnaise

Directions

Preheat oven to 400F.

Oil small individual oven proof dishes, or use one large dish. Remove the fish from fridge and let come to room temperature.

In a bowl mix together the garlic, pine nuts, cheese, pesto and mayonnaise.

Place the fish in the oil dish and spoon the pine nut mixture over the top ensuring it is evenly coated.

Use all the mixture and make spreading as thick as possible.

Bake in oven for 12-15 minutes, the fish should be firm to the touch and the crust should be browned.

Serve hot with a side salad.

Ingredients: Serves 4

4 tilapia, fillets
4 cloves garlic, crushed or finely chopped
3 tbsp olive oil
1 onion, finely chopped
1 tbsp cayenne pepper
Salt and Pepper

Directions

Lay the fish fillets in an oven proof dish. Rub them well with the crushed garlic.

Drizzle with the olive oil until well coated. Evenly lay the onion across the fillets.

Cover and refrigerate overnight or at least 6 hours.

Preheat oven to 350F

Remove fish from oven. Sprinkle with cayenne, salt and pepper. Let fish come to room temperature, about 30 minutes.

Bake for 30 minutes.

Honey Ginger Salmon

Ingredients: Serves 4

4 salmon individual small fillets
2 red onions, finely chopped
1 garlic clove, finely chopped
3 tsp olive oil
2 tbsp honey
2 tsp grated fresh ginger
1.5 tsp hot sauce

Directions

Preheat oven to 350F.

Using 1 tablespoon of oil, coat an oven proof dish.

Lay the salmon fillets on this, surround with the onion and garlic.

Sprinkle the ginger and hot sauce over everything. Drizzle the honey evenly over the fillets.

Bake for 20 minutes.

Serve over risotto. Use the juices in the oven proof dish to flavour the risotto once ready.

Zucchini Pasta

Ingredients: Serves 2

3 Zucchini, longer is better
2 tbsp of olive oil
½ tsp of salt
½ tsp of lemon peel
2 tbsp of chopped basil
¼ can of chopped tomatoes
1 tsp paprika
1 tbsp minced garlic
Parmesan cheese to taste, grated

Directions

Remove the ends of the zucchini and julienne. Throw away the core and seeds as they don't sauté well.

Place a pan over a medium heat add 1 tablespoon of oil and the garlic. Cook the garlic for 2 minutes before adding the tomatoes, paprika.
Bring to a boil and let simmer for 15 minutes.

Whilst simmering put a large pan over a medium-heat heat and add 1 tablespoon of oil. Add the zucchini, salt and lemon peel. Toss well and cook for 3 -4 minutes.

1-2 minutes into cooking add the chopped basil and continue to cook until zucchini is soft.

Turn off the heat and add the tomato sauce to the zucchini. Toss well.

Sprinkle parmesan and serve.

Polenta & Butter Bean Stew

Ingredients: Serves 2-4

4 tsp olive oil, divided
1 16 oz. tube prepared plain polenta, cut into smallish cubes
1 clove garlic, minced or finely chopped
1 onion, thinly sliced
1 red bell pepper, chopped
½ tsp paprika, plus more for garnish
1 can butter beans, rinsed
4 cups baby spinach
¾ cup vegetable broth
½ cup shredded cheese
2 tsp sherry vinegar

Directions

Put a pan over a medium-high heat and add 2 teaspoons of oil.

Add polenta cubes and cook, stirring occasionally. After 8-10 minutes they should be well browned. Take out of pan.

Reduce heat to medium and add the rest of the oil. Add the garlic and onion to pan and cook for 2 minutes.

Throw in the pepper and continue to cook for 3 minutes.

Sprinkle with paprika and toss well.

Add the beans, vegetable broth and spinach. Continue to stir and cook for a further 4 minutes.

Take off the heat and add the cheese and vinegar. Stir well.

Serve over green boiled green vegetables. Add more paprika to taste.

Ingredients: Serve 4

¼ cup olive oil
3 tbsp minced garlic
Zest from 2 lemons
Splash of dry white win
2 tbsp freshly squeezed lemon juice
1.5 tsp dried oregano
1 tsp minced fresh thyme leaves
Sea salt and ground black pepper
4 boneless chicken breasts, ideally with skin on
1 lemon, halved

Directions

Preheat oven to 400F

Put a small pan over a medium heat and warm the olive oil. Add the garlic, cook for 30 seconds.

Take off the heat and add white wine, zest, lemon juice, oregano, thyme and salt. Mix well.

Pour into an oven proof dish. Place the chicken breasts skin side up on top of the sauce.

Drizzle the breasts with olive oil and sprinkle with salt and pepper. Cut the lemon into wedges and place them around and over the chicken.

Bake for 35 minutes, or until done.

If the top hasn't browned, switch oven to broiler and leave to brown for 3 minutes.

Remove from oven, cover and leave to rest for 10 minutes.

Serve and use the juice from the dish as a sauce.

Nutty Chickpea & Carrot Salad

Ingredients: Serves 4

1 red onion, sliced
1 can chickpeas, drained
4 carrots, shaved
2 garlic cloves, finely chopped
¼ cup pinenuts
2 tbsp white wine vinegar
Salt and pepper to taste
2 tbsp olive oil

Directions

Add oil to a pan and place over a medium heat.

Add the red onion, garlic, chickpeas and cook for 3 minutes.

Add the carrots and pine nuts, cook for another 2 minutes.
Drizzle with vinegar, season with salt and pepper.

Chicken Saltimbocca

Ingredients: Serves 4-6

4 chicken breasts, pounded flat
1.5 cups fresh spinach
4 slices of prosciutto or Parma ham
1 cup of gluten-free chicken stock
½ cup grated Parmesan
3 tbsp olive oil
1.5 tsp freshly chopped rosemary
1.5 tsp pepper
1.5 tsp salt
Juice from one lemon
Toothpicks or kitchen string

Directions

Add the spinach to small bowl and toss with 1 tbsp olive oil and ½ tsp each of salt and pepper. Set this aside for now.

Take the flattened breasts and lay them out and sprinkle with the remainder of the salt and pepper.

Lay a slice of prosciutto over each piece of chicken and arrange some spinach leaves on top. Sprinkle rosemary & Parmesan over everything.

Roll up the chicken ensuring that the stuffing stays tucked inside. Once rolled up secure the chicken with a toothpick (or tie together with string).

Heat the remaining olive oil over a medium heat in a saucepan. Add chicken and for cook 2-3 minutes per side or until golden brown.

Add the stock and lemon juice to the pan and slowly bring to a boil over the medium heat.

Once boiling point is reached reduce the heat, cover, and let it simmer for 5 minutes longer. Ensure the chicken is now cooked through, if not cook for a further 1-2 minutes.

Take the chicken from pan, remove the toothpicks and let rest.

Increase heat on pan and stir the sauce until it reduces, 5 more minutes or so will suffice.

Pour the sauce over the chicken or serve on the side.

Ingredients: Serves 4-6

4 gluten-free chicken breast
1 cup almonds
¼ cup grated parmesan cheese
1 tsp sea salt
1 tsp black pepper
4 tbsp olive oil
4 tbsp butter (unsalted)
½ cup gluten-free chicken stock
3 tbsp lemon juice
¼ cup capers, drained
¼ cup parsley, roughly chopped
2 lemons

Directions

Pound the chicken breasts flat.

Put almonds in blender or processor and pulse until they turn into a fine meal. Do not turn it to a paste.

Add the cheese, salt and pepper to processor and pulse a few more times to mix everything together.

Put the mixture on a large flat plate or surface and spread out.

Rinse the chicken in water and let the excess drip off. Chicken should be damp. Now dredge the chicken in the almond mixture, pressing the mixture onto both sides of the chicken.

Heat a large pan over medium high heat and add the olive oil and 2 tbsp of butter.

Once the oil is heated and the butter melted, place chicken breasts in the pan. Cooking for 3-4 minutes per side or until well browned.

Remove chicken breasts to a serving dish and cover to them keep warm. Place in a warm oven, not a hot oven.

Add chicken stock and lemon juice to the pan. Scrape the pan with spatula to incorporate all the browned bits of almond paste.

Add the capers and cook over medium heat until the sauce is reduced by half.

Switch off heat add the remaining butter and stir well.

Pour the sauce over the chicken and garnish with chopped parsley.
Serve with wedges on the side.

Simple Italian Meatballs

Ingredients: Serves 4-6

1 pound ground beef, lean is best
1 cup gluten-free crackers, crushed
2 eggs
1 tsp oregano
½ tsp garlic powder
½ tsp salt
½ cup parmesan cheese

Directions

Mix all the ingredients together in a large bowl. Using your hands is best way to do this.

Form the mixture roughly into balls, ensure not to press too hard together or the meatballs will taste dry.

Place balls on a greased baking sheet and bake in oven at 400F for 20 - 30 minutes, turning once after 10-15 minutes.

Heat your go –to gluten free marinara sauce in a sauce pan and bring to a simmer.

Add the meatballs and bring back to a simmer for 10 minutes.

Parmesan & Eggplant Bake

Ingredients: Serves 4-6

2 eggplants, peeled and cut into rounds
2 eggs whisked with 2 tbsp of milk
1 cup gluten-free bread crumbs
48 oz. marinara sauce
1.5 cups of mozzarella cheese
2 tbsp Olive oil
Gluten-free spaghetti

Directions

Preheat oven to 375F

Grease two baking sheets with olive oil.

Put the whisked eggs in a bowl and spread the bread crumbs on large plate.

Dip the eggplant rounds in the egg and then coat with breadcrumbs. Place the breaded rounds on the baking sheets.

Repeat until all rounds are breaded and placed on baking sheets.

Bake for 40 minutes and turning half way through.

Whilst doing this take your marinara sauce and begin to heat in a pan until it simmers.

Turn the oven temperature up to 400F.

Pour 2 cups of the sauce into a baking dish. Layer the eggplant over the sauce and then cover the eggplant with more sauce. Top with mozzarella cheese sprinkled over the top.

Repeat with any remaining eggplant and sauce, making new layers until finished.

Bake for 15-20 minutes. Serve over spaghetti.

Ingredients: Serves 4

12 oz. gluten free pasta, I use penne
1 jar of sun-dried tomato pesto
1 cup of fresh green beans, cut
2 or 3 potatoes, medium sized, diced
2 tbsp olive oil

Directions

Boil the potatoes and beans together for until tender. About 10-15 minutes.

Cook the pasta according to the package directions.

Drain the pasta, the potatoes and the beans.

Heat a pan over a medium heat and add the oil.

Add the pasta, green beans, potatoes, and pesto together and toss well.

Grate parmesan over before serving.

Shrimp & Spinach Bake

Ingredients: Serves 4-6

2 tbsp olive oil
2 cups frozen shelled shrimp
5 cloves garlic, minched
2 tbsp chopped basil
Black pepper to taste
1.5 tbsp balsamic vinegar
2 cups of cooked brown rice
16 oz. frozen spinach, drained and thawed
½ cup of sweet grape tomatoes, halved
½ tsp nutmeg
Sea salt
6 oz. garlic and herb marinated mozzarella, sliced

Directions

Preheat the oven to 350F.

In a large pan heat a little olive oil over a medium heat and add the shrimp and garlic. Stir them for 2 minutes.

Switch off the heat, add balsamic and mix well.

In a baking dish make a layer of the cooked rice at the bottom. Add the chopped spinach evenly over the top. Sprinkle with the nutmeg, sea salt and pepper. Add half of the grape tomatoes.

Create a layer with half of the mozzarella.

The next layer is made up of the shrimp, ensure it is distributed evenly. Pour any remaining garlic oil over the top.

Add the rest of the tomatoes and top with the remaining mozzarella.

Cover and bake for 30 minutes.

.

Chicken with Balsamic Peppers

Ingredients: Serves 4-6

4 large bell peppers
1 large onion, chopped finely
⅓ cup balsamic vinegar
1 tbsp gluten-free Worcestershire Sauce
¼ cup olive oil
¼ cup gluten-free chicken broth
6 cloves of garlic, chopped
1 tbsp dry basil
½ tsp thyme
½ tsp rosemary
4 chicken breasts
Sea salt and ground pepper, to taste

Directions

Preheat oven to 375F.

Add the pepper and onion slices into a large bowl. Add the balsamic vinegar, Worcestershire, olive oil, broth, garlic and herbs, toss well with peppers and onions.

Place the chicken breasts in the bottom of a baking pan coated with olive oil. Season with salt and pepper to your taste. Pour the balsamic pepper mixture over the chicken and arrange evenly.

Loosely cover the pan and place in your oven. Bake for 20 minutes.

Take out the pan and spoon the sauce over the chicken breasts to keep them moist.

Cover again and bake for another 10-20 minutes, you're wanting to make it as tender as possible.

Serve with a side dish of rice, quinoa or gluten-free pasta tossed in pesto.

Mushroom Risotto with a Twist

Ingredients: Serves 4

6 cups gluten-free chicken broth
3 tbsp butter, in small pieces
2 tbsp olive oil
1 pound Portobello mushrooms, thinly sliced
1 pound porcini mushrooms, thinly sliced
2 shallots, chopped
1 garlic clove, minced
2 cups Arborio rice
⅓ cup dry white wine
3 tbsp chopped chives
2 tbsp chopped parsley
2 tbsp lemon juice
4 tsp grated lemon peel
1 cup grated Parmesan cheese
Sea salt to taste
Black pepper to taste

Directions

In a saucepan, warm the broth over a low heat.

In a medium pot, heat 2 tbsp olive oil, over medium heat. Add the mushrooms, and cook until soft, about 3 minutes. Remove the mushrooms and liquid, set aside.

Add 1 tbsp olive oil to the pan, and stir in the shallots. Cook for 1 minute until shallots are clear. Add the garlic and cook for 2 minutes.

Add the rice and stir well until coated. Cook for 2 minutes.

Pour in wine, stirring continually until the wine is fully absorbed. Add 1/2 cup of broth to the rice, and stir until the broth is absorbed.

Continue adding broth 1/2 cup at a time, stirring continuously, until the liquid is absorbed and the rice is cooked. Should take 15 – 20 minutes.

Remove from the heat, and stir in the butter, mushrooms and mushroom liquid, parsley, chives, lemon juice, lemon peel and Parmesan.

Season with salt and pepper to taste.

Pea Risotto with Mint

Ingredients: Serves 4

1.5 cups Arborio rice
1 cup frozen peas, thawed
2 tbsp fresh mint, roughly chopped
1 onion, diced
2 cloves garlic, minced
4 tbsp butter
1 cup white wine
4 cups gluten-free chicken broth
½ cup grated Parmesan cheese
Salt and pepper to taste

Directions

In a small saucepan heat the broth over medium heat until warm.

Take 2 tablespoons butter and melt in a medium pan. Add the onions and garlic and cook until soft, about 5 minutes.

Add the rice and cook for about 2 minutes. Ensure everything is well coated.

Add the wine and cook until liquid is absorbed, stirring frequently for about 5 minutes.

Ladle ½ cup of broth into rice and cook until absorbed.

Repeat ½ cup at a time until rice is cooked but still firm, should take about 20-25 minutes.

Fold in the peas and remove from heat.

Add cheese and mint and fold once or twice.

Season with salt and pepper before serving.

Beef & Mushroom Chilli Stew

Ingredients: Serves 4-6

1 tbsp olive oil
½ red onion, diced
5 cloves garlic, chopped
1 pound ground beef
2 cups mushrooms, chopped
1 bell pepper, seeds and core removed, sliced
¼ tsp cumin
¼ tsp nutmeg
½ tsp red pepper
2 tomatoes, seeded, diced
2 tsp mixed Italian herbs - basil, oregano, marjoram, sage, thyme
1 tbsp of balsamic vinegar
1 tbsp raw agave nectar
¼ cup gluten-free Ketchup
½ cup of gluten-free beef broth
Chopped parsley

Directions

Heat olive oil in a large pan under a medium heat and add the onion and garlic. Stir for a minute or two.

Add the ground beef, mushrooms, peppers, tomatoes. Add spices and herbs, stir well. Add more to your personal taste if you want.

Cook until the meat is browned then add the balsamic, agave and ketchup. Stir well.

Keep pan on a low simmer and it take off the heat once all the pinkness leaves the meat.

Add the broth and continue to cook in the pan on a low simmer. Once the broth is absorbed switch off the heat.

Sprinkle with some fresh chopped parsley to serve.

Caramelized Butternut Squash Cubes

Ingredients: Serves 4

2 medium butternut squashes
1 large onion, chopped finely
6 - 8 tbsp butter (unsalted), melted
¼ cup brown sugar
1-5 tsp sea salt
Black pepper to taste

Directions

Preheat the oven to 400F.

Cut off the ends of each butternut squash and discard.

Peel the squash and cut in half lengthwise. You will need a sharp, heavy knife for this.

Remove the seeds.

Cut the squash into cubes and put in large mixing bowl.

Add the onion, melted butter, brown sugar, salt and pepper. Toss ingredients well.

Spread out the ingredients in a single layer on the baking sheet.

Put in oven for 45 minutes to 55 minutes, until the squash is tender and the glaze begins to caramelize.

Turn the squash while roasting to be sure it browns evenly.

Adjust seasonings to personal taste.

Ingredients

200g gluten-free flour
½ salt
2 tbsp olive oil
7g sachet fast-action dried yeast
1 tbsp chopped rosemary
1 tsp ground black pepper
125-150ml warm water
2 cups grated mozzarella
210g jar tomatoes bruschetta topping

Topping suggestions. Pick & Choose.
Mozzarella, torn
Avocado
Cherry tomatoes, cut
Parma ham
Chopped ham
Chopped pineapple
Olive oil
Balsamic vinegar

Directions

Heat oven to 430F.

Put the flour, salt, olive oil, yeast, rosemary and pepper into a food processor. Pulse until everything is well mixed.

Turn the motor to its slowest speed and slowly add just enough water to bring the flour to a soft dough.

Empty the contents out onto a work surface dusted with flour and knead until it comes together.

Halve the dough and roll out each half on oiled baking sheets into very thin 25cm or 10 inch rounds. There is no need to form a rim at the edge.

Spoon the tomato topping onto each dough round (don't spread to the very edge).

Sprinkle the grated cheese over the top.

Leave to stand for 15 minutes before baking in the oven for 12-15 minutes. The dough should be crisp.

Use the fresh topping suggestions and make the pizza just how you like it.

Flaked Fish in Lemon Lentils

Ingredients: Serves 2-3

4 oz. Lentils, Puy are best
1 onion, finely chopped
1 carrot, finely chopped
1 celery stick, finely chopped
½ pint vegetable stock
1 rounded tbsp half-fat crème fraiche
2 tbsp chopped dill
The zest of ½ a lemon
2 x 4oz any white fish fillets
2oz. baby spinach leaves

Directions

Add lentils into an oiled pan with the chopped onion, carrot and celery and place over a medium heat.

Add the stock and bring to the boil. Stir a few times and reduce the heat. Cover and let simmer for 20-25 minutes. The lentils should be tender after this time.

In a bowl mix together the crème fraiche, half the dill and the lemon zest, adding a little seasoning, to taste.

Put the fillets in a shallow microwave proof dish with a splash of water and cover with cling film leaving one corner open slightly.

Microwave on medium for 4-6 minutes until the fish flakes easily when touched with a fork. Flake the fish with a fork.

Once the lentils are tender, add the spinach and stir. Continue to cook at a low heat and add the crème fraiche once the spinach has wilted.

Serve between 2-3 plates and top with flaked fish. Garnish with the remaining dill.

Pasta with a Walnut Pesto

Ingredients: Serves 4

Walnut Pesto
25g walnut pieces
2 garlic cloves, minced
Zest of 1 large lemon
25g parsley
4 tbsp olive oil

Pasta
2 red onions, quartered and separated into pieces
1 tbsp olive oil
250ml pack gluten-free pasta
250g jar of mixed peppers, drained and chopped roughly
50g parmesan cheese, grated

Directions

Put the walnuts, garlic and lemon zest into a food processor and pulse until chopped.

Add the parsley and oil and pulse again to combine everything together.

Season to taste.

Preheat grill to high.

Add the onions to a grill pan, sprinkle with 1 tbsp oil and toss to coat.

Arrange in a single layer and grill for 6-8 minutes until lightly browned.

As the onions cook begin to cook the pasta according to the pack instructions.

Drain the pasta.

In a large sauce pan, add a splash of olive oil and heat on medium. Add the pesto, cooked onions, peppers and stir for 1 minute.

Add the drained pasta and stir well. Sprinkle with parmesan.

White Bean Gnocchi

Ingredients: Serves 4

1 tbsp olive oil
2 garlic cloves, minced
3 cups white beans
¼ tsp sea salt
1 can vegetable broth
1 box or pack of gluten-free gnocchi
2 tbsp chopped basil
¼ tsp lemon zest
¼ tsp pepper
1 tsp fresh lemon juice

Directions

In a large pan, heat olive oil over a medium heat.

Add the garlic and cook for 2 minutes, until it is golden brown. Pour in the white beans, salt and vegetable broth. Cook this at a simmer for 20 minutes stirring occasionally.

Cook the gnocchi according to package directions.

Once the gnocchi is cooked remove from heat and drain.

Add this to the white bean mixture and cook for a further 1 minute, stirring occasionally.

Remove from heat and add the basil and lemon zest.

Stuffed Mushrooms

Ingredients

4 mushroom caps, Portobello is best
¼ tsp salt
¼ tsp pepper
1 cup ricotta cheese
1 cup spinach, chopped finely
½ cup Parmesan cheese, shredded
2 tbsp chopped black olives, de-stoned and chopped finely
½ tsp Italian seasoning
¾ cup marinara sauce

Directions

Preheat oven to 450°F.

Take a baking tray and grease with oil.

Place the mushroom, gill side up on the tray and sprinkle with salt and pepper to taste.

Bake for 20-25 minutes.

In a large bowl mix together and mash the ricotta, spinach, ¼ cup parmesan, chopped olives, Italian seasoning and the remaining small amount of pepper in a medium bowl.

Microwave the marinara sauce in a bowl until piping hot. Don't forget to cover it before.

When the mushrooms are finished cooking, pour out any liquid in the caps by turning gill side down.

Return the mushrooms to the tray gill side up and put 1 tbsp marinara into each cap.

Spoon ricotta onto the marinara sauce and sprinkle with the remaining parmesan.

Return to oven and bake for 10 minutes. Serve with the remaining sauce drizzled atop.

Ingredients: Serves 4-6

24 whole cherry peppers
1 can of tuna, drain well before use
1 tbsp lemon juice
1 tbsp olive oil
1 tbsp capers, rinsed and finely chopped
2 anchovy fillets, finely chopped
Black pepper to taste
¼ cup balsamic vinegar

Directions

Take peppers and prepare by removing stems and scooping out seeds.

Add the tuna, lemon juice, oil, capers and anchovies in a bowl. Mix together.

Pack each pepper with the tuna mix and put them on your serving plate.

Grind some pepper over the peppers.

In a saucepan add the balsamic vinegar and simmer until reduced to about 2 tsp. It should take you about 2-3 minutes.

Using a teaspoon drizzle the syrup over the peppers and serve.

Simple Roasted & Spiced Chicken Tenders

Ingredients: Serves 4

½ tsp grated lemon zest
3 tbsp lemon juice
2 tbsp garlic, finely chopped or minced
1 tsp dried oregano
2 tbsp finely chopped jalapeno peppers
2 tbsp olive oil
½ tsp salt
1 pound of chicken tenders, or breasts sliced lengthwise.
1 bell pepper, seeds removed and thinly sliced
½ onion, thinly sliced

Directions

Preheat oven to 425F.

Mix together the lemon zest, lemon juice, garlic, oregano, jalapenos, oil and salt in a bowl.

Add the chicken, pepper and onion to the bowl and toss to coat thoroughly.

On a baking tray spread the chicken tenders out evenly and cover with foil.

Bake for about 25 minutes, or until the chicken is cooked through.

Chicken & Sausage Stew

Ingredients: Serves 4

2 tbsp butter, unsalted
1 pound chicken breasts, cut into medium sized chunks
½ pound Italian sausage, cut into medium sized chunks
½ pound hot Italian sausage, cut into medium sized chunks
1 tbsp potato flour
1 onion, chopped finely
1 red pepper sliced
1 green pepper, sliced
3 cloves garlic, minced
½ cup red wine
¾ cup gluten-free chicken broth
⅓ cup Parmesan grated
¼ cup finely chopped Italian parsley
Sea salt and black pepper to taste
2 pickled cherry peppers, chopped, plus 2 tbsp of the liquid
from the jar

Directions

Heat 1 tbsp butter in a large pan over medium to high heat

Once the butter begins to melt add the sausage and cook until
it is golden brown. Turn off the heat and set aside.

Season the chicken with salt and pepper and dredge in the
potato flour.

Add another tbsp of butter to the pan and turn heat to medium.

Place the chicken in the pan and cook for about 3 minutes per
side, until browned, but not cooked all the way through.

Add the onion, peppers, garlic, ½ teaspoon salt, and pepper to
taste and cook for 3 minutes.

Now add the wine to the pan and bring to a boil. Turn the heat down and cook until it begins to reduce.

Add the broth, increase the heat slightly and bring back to a simmer.

Cover and let simmer for 5 minutes.

Move the chicken, sausage and vegetables to a plate or dish. Ensure the chicken and sausage is cooked through.

Turn the heat to high and stir in the parsley and cherry peppers and their liquid into the pan.

Boil until reduced by a third. Remove from the heat and stir in the remaining 1 tbsp butter.

Pour the sauce and cherry pepper mixture over the chicken, sausage and vegetables.

Serve atop rice and sprinkle with parmesan cheese.

Chicken Cacciatore

Ingredients: Serves 4-6

4 chicken thighs
2 chicken breasts, cut in half
½ cup of potato starch, for dredging
3 tbsp olive oil
1 green pepper, sliced
1 red pepper, sliced
1 onion, sliced
4 garlic cloves, minced
¾ cup dry white wine
1 can of diced tomatoes
¾ cup gluten-free chicken broth
3 tbsp capers, drained
1.5 tsp dried oregano leaves
¼ cup chopped basil leaves
2.5 tsp salt
1.5 tsp black pepper

Directions

Take the chicken pieces and sprinkle with 1 tsp of salt and pepper. Dredge the chicken pieces in potato starch to coat lightly.

In a large pan, heat the oil over a medium heat. When the oil is heated add the dredged chicken and cook until brown, about 5 minutes per side.

Take the chicken from the pan and set aside.

In the same pan sauté the pepper, onion and garlic over a medium heat for 5-6 minutes. Season with salt and pepper to your taste as you cook.

Pour in the wine in and let it simmer for a few minutes until the liquid is reduced by half.

Add the tomatoes (along with the juice in the can), chicken broth, capers and oregano. Stir well.

Return the chicken pieces to the pan and stir until they are well coated. Return the sauce to a simmer.

Continue to simmer over a low heat until the chicken is cooked through. Should take 25-30 minutes.

If the sauce isn't thick enough remove the chicken and increase the heat until it thickens.

Serve with gluten free pasta or rice.

Cheese Risotto

Ingredients: Serves 4

1 quart gluten-free chicken stock
1.5 cups Arborio rice
½ cup white wine
1 shallot, chopped
3 tbsp of butter, unsalted
⅓ cup grated Parmesan cheese
1.5 tbsp Italian parsley, chopped
1 tbsp olive oil
Salt and pepper, to taste

Directions

In a medium pan heat the stock to a simmer and then reduce heat to low.

In a separate pan heat the oil and 1 tbsp of butter over a medium heat. As the butter melts add the shallot and cook for 3 minutes.

Add the rice to the pan and stir it with a wooden spoon or heat-proof spatula. Don't use a fork or metal spatula. Ensure the rice is well coated.

Ensuring not to let the rice get browned in the pan cook for another 1-2 minutes.

Pour in the wine, and continue to stir and cook until the rice completely absorbs the liquid.

When the rice begins to appear dry add a ladle of hot chicken stock to the rice and stir until the liquid is fully absorbed.

When the rice looks to be nearly dry again add another ladle of stock and repeat the process.

It's very important to keep stirring the rice while cooking stock to keep it from burning.

One ladle at a time, keep adding stock and stirring the rice until the liquid is absorbed. As it cooks, the rice will become creamy as the starches begin to escape.

Keep adding stock, one ladle at a time, for 20-30 minutes. The rice should be tender by the point. If you run out of stock, use hot water.

Stir in the remaining 2 tbsp of butter, the parmesan cheese and the parsley, and season with salt and pepper.

Spoon the risotto into mounds on your serving plates, it shouldn't be runny, and sprinkle with Parmesan cheese

Dessert Recipes

Raspberry Flutes with a Choco Crunch

Ingredients: Serves 4

250g raspberries
2 tbsp Cointreau
Zest and juice from 1 small orange
100g gluten free, chocolate
3 tbsp soya milk
50g caster sugar
6 tbsp gluten, wheat and nut-free muesli

Directions

Split the raspberries between 4 champagne glasses.

Pour ½ tbsp of Cointreau and a little orange zest and juice over each, then set the glasses aside.

In a small pot melt the chocolate, under a low heat, stir in the soya milk and set aside off the heat.

In a new pot, add the sugar along with 3 tbsp of water. Over a low to medium heat, cook without stirring for about 7 minutes until the sugar starts to melts and turns golden brown. Now add the muesli and stir in

Pour out onto a tray lined with baking parchment.

Leave to cool, then smash or crush into thin shards.

Pour the chocolate mixture between the glasses and allow to cool, at room temperature.

Scatter over the caramel crunch to serve.

Carrot Cake

Ingredients: Serves 4

140g butter, unsalted and softened
200g caster sugar
250g carrots, grated
140g sultanas
2 eggs, lightly beaten
200g gluten-free self-rising flour
1 tsp cinnamon
1 tsp gluten-free baking powder
50g mixed nuts, roughly chopped

For the icing
75g butter, unsalted and softened
175g icing sugar
3 tsp cinnamon, plus extra for dusting

Directions

Heat oven to 350F.

Grease and line a loaf tin with baking paper.

Whisk the butter and sugar together in a mixing bowl.

Add the grated carrot and sultanas, stir together. Crack the eggs and whisk everything well. Ensure the eggs are fully separated.

Add the flour, cinnamon, baking powder and most of the nuts and mix well.

Pour the mix into the loaf tin and bake for 55 minutes. A good sign of it being ready is when a skewer poked through the middle comes out clean.

Allow to cool in the tin for 15 minutes then remove and let cool completely.

As it cools begin to make the icing.

Beat the butter in a large bowl until soft, add the icing sugar and cinnamon, then beat until thick and creamy.

When the cake is fully cooled, spread the icing on top. Sprinkle with a little cinnamon and the remaining chopped nuts.

Hazelnut Cookies

Ingredients: Serves 6-8

2 cups hazelnuts, toasted
¼ cups sugar
4 large egg whites
½ tsp salt
1 tsp vanilla extract

Directions

Preheat the oven to 325F

Take two 2 baking trays and line with greased parchment paper. Set up oven so both racks are close to centre as possible.

Add the nuts and sugar to a food processor and pulse until they finely ground. Transfer into a mixing bowl.

Whisk the egg whites and salt in another bowl with an electric hand mixer on high speed until stiff peaks begin to form.

Using a spatula fold the egg whites into the nut mixture.

Add vanilla and mix together gently until well combined.

Drop the batter by using a tablespoon onto the baking trays and leave a 2 inch gap between batter drops.

Add to the oven and bake until golden brown. It should take 25 minutes. If you don't own a fan assisted oven be sure to rotate the position of the baking trays in the oven.

Remove from oven and let cool for 5 minutes.

Transfer the cookies to a wire rack to cool completely.

Repeat until batter is complete.

Chocolate Gelato

(Don't have an ice cream maker? Check out the free gift at the front of the book)

Ingredients: Serves 4

½ cup unsweetened cocoa powder
2 14 oz. cans coconut milk, divided
1 tsp vanilla extract
¾ cup plus 2 tbsp sugar
2 tbsp corn-starch
⅛ tsp salt

Directions

Put cocoa in a medium bowl and whisk in ⅔ of a cup coconut milk until it makes a smooth paste. Once paste is created add the vanilla and stir in.

In a medium saucepan mix together the sugar, corn-starch and salt.

Gradually whisk in the rest of the coconut milk. Heat over a medium heat, stirring frequently until the mixture gets close to simmering.

Let simmer for 2.5 to 3 minutes.

Scrape the hot mixture into the bowl with the cocoa mixture.

Whisk until well blended. Let cool for about 40 minutes and then cover and refrigerate until cold.

Pour the mixture into your ice cream maker and freeze according to machine directions.

Coffee & Brandy Panna-Cotta

Ingredients: Serving – depends on container size

Panna-Cotta
1 cup hot coffee
1 envelope unflavored gelatin (about 2 ¼ tsp)
¾ cup vanilla yogurt, non-fat is best
¾ cup milk
2 tsp brandy
½ tsp vanilla extract
¼ tsp ground cinnamon
⅓ cup granulated sugar
½ cup whipping cream
Brandy Sauce
3 tbsp brown sugar
3 tbsp brewed coffee
2 tbsp brandy

Directions

To prepare the panna-cotta:

Place ¼ cup of hot coffee in a heat-proof bowl. Sprinkle the gelatin over the coffee and stir to mix. Let it stand for 5 minutes until it cools to warm.

Whisk the remaining coffee, the yogurt, milk, 2 tsp brandy, vanilla and cinnamon in a bowl.

Microwave the coffee and gelatin mixture, uncovered, until the gelatin has completely dissolved. Ensure it doesn't boil though.

Add the sugar and stir it until it is dissolved.

Slowly mix the gelatin-coffee into the yogurt mixture. Refrigerate this and stir occasionally, until it just begins to thicken – about 30 to 45 minutes.

Whisk the cream with an electric mixer or whisk until peaks begin to form.

Mix into the yogurt mixture and whisk until smooth.

Divide among small containers such as ramekins.

Cover and refrigerate until the panna-cotta is set. 24 hours is the perfect time for this but less will suffice.

To prepare sauce:

In a pan add the brown sugar and 3 tbsp of coffee. Bring this to the boil over a medium heat and ensure you are continually stirring. Once the liquid is reduced by half remove from the heat.

Add 2 tbsp of brandy and use a grill lighter to ignite the liquid. Shake the pan gently until the flames cook off.

To serve:

Make the sauce just before you are ready to serve.

Remove the panna-cottas from fridge 1-5 minutes before.

Drizzle each panna-cotta dish with the coffee brandy sauce.

Made in the USA
Middletown, DE
30 January 2020